Jeffrey Cyphers Wright

FUEL FOR LOVE

SV

SurVision Books

First published in 2024 by
SurVision Books
Dublin, Ireland
Reggio di Calabria, Italy
www.survisionmagazine.com

Copyright © Jeffrey Cyphers Wright, 2024

Cover image from Dall-e (AI) prompt: "The marriage of a mirage and a carriage, Sean Landers style" by the author

Design © SurVision Books, 2024

ISBN: 978-1-912963-45-4

This book is in copyright. No part of this publication may be reproduced, stored in a retrieval system, or transmitted in any form or by any means without the prior permission in writing from the publisher.

Acknowledgments

Grateful acknowledgment is made to the editors of the following, in which some of these poems, or versions of them, originally appeared.

The journals: *Big Hammer, The Café Review, Clockwise Cat, Fell Swoop, First Literary Review East, The Hurricane Review, Live Mag!, Lonesome, North of Oxford, Spillwords, Stat-o-Rec,* and *SurVision.*

The anthologies: *The Best American Poetry* (ed. by David Lehman and Elaine Equi, Scribner, 2023); *Contemporary Surrealist and Magical Realist Poetry: An International Anthology* (ed. by Jonas Zdanys, Lamar University Literary Press, 2022); *NYC From the Inside* (ed. by George Wallace, Blue Light Press, 2022); *Contemporary Tangential Surrealist Poetry: An Anthology* (ed. by Tony Kitt, SurVision Books, 2023); *Brevitas 20 2023 Anthology of the Short Poem* (ed. by Ron Kolm, Brevitas, 2023); *The Arcade of the Scribes / Arcada de los Escribos* (ed. by C.D. Johnson, Rogue Scholars Press, 2023).

CONTENTS

The Quick Key	5
Ghost Powder	6
Giant Sighs	7
Sweepstake	8
Paradise Answering Service	9
Hyperion Takes a Hit	10
Peter the Great	11
Spreading the Wealth	12
Shame and the Shamans	13
State Mint	14
Cantata	15
The Ostrich Colony	16
Ode to a Nightcap	17
Required Fields	18
Ask Me	19
Changing Station	20
Host and Hostage	21
Fog's Heavy Crown	22
Salvos	23
Sexistentialism	24
Fuel for Love	25
Tall King Talking	26
The Daily News	27
Glad to Be of Surface	28
The Wichita Doctors Are Restless	29
White Toaster	30
Custer's Last Dessert	31
Placeholder	32
Calling the Tune	33
Nights & Daisies	34

The Quick Key

Ever-shrinking path to glory's kennel,
sunset's corsage smudges the Hudson.

Cormorants command black pilings.
Loneliness spreads grape kush wings.

Who says you have to work late?
Who insists you flirt with posterity?

Time races on in a black Thunderbird,
ashes knocking at the fire door.

Who says you need to guard the EXIT?
A burning submarine fingering the sea.

Fun melts away as you polish light,
chasing the hounds of fame.

Razor-thin euphoria is a wake-up call.
The party is here—inside these cells.

Ghost Powder

A few clouds scallop the sky like pale fish
over the river. The carousel on Pier 25
closes for the season. I waste my days
courting puppets and chasing women.
October turns out its empty pockets,
squeezing the last glow from evening.

The nation teeters on spindly hind legs.
I almost lose it in the Bureau of Frustration.
Baz and I swap jail stories at Howl!
The pigeon lady quivers under feathers
at Union Square. Katherine Bradford
paints a pirate ship in my imagination.

Another friend had a stroke.
The frogs have a motto: "Born to croak."

Giant Sighs

August is a saucy scamp, a brazen hustler,
rustling in black silk and fishnet stockings.
In purple dahlia. Dianthus laced with Apollo.

August is a racehorse in a cave. A county fair.
Boiling-over light in the warehouse of desire.
Antlers on a heatwave. A wedding caked.

Shopping for memories, sumptuous red
trumpet vines tumble over the fence line.
You coin a word to quell the nerve-swell:

Troubadourable. Busier than a Byzantine.
The herald arrives eerily early. Dire portents
gather up steam for the Monster Prom.

Truth shuttles through a stuttering loom.
And August swaggers, drunk on the moon.

Sweepstake

Garlic paper flakes off like dried seconds
impatient for me to anoint them.
I whirl through the month, a dizzy twister.
Not every day is a holiday. You don't say?

A genie rises from the bowl. Smoke signals.
Coffee holds out a brown mitten.
We grind the candle light, smelting ardor.
An aqua tug bullies its cargo upstream.

Plenty to take care of here. Plenty to share.
Trains leave every hour but we stay.
Glinting wires hint at the unseen
guides that keep our act gliding on air.

The river slips from steel into teal satin.
Dusk's push broom comes, sweeping us on.

Paradise Answering Service

November draws its purse strings tight.
The moon is eaten by a pack of clouds.
My old lamp blinks, its wiring worn out.

Between useless and euphoria, I sleuth
for meaning, meandering from Chelsea
to the river. Listening to The Shivers ...

to Robert Kelly lifting scripture off
a mirror. On Windmill Attack Mode.
Milling around in my grab bag of genes.

At the end, the language we suspend
will sheperd us past midnight's derrick.
Leaning on eternity like a vagrant. O,

I'll still pay for the foolish love I spent
when you were on top of my to-do list.

Hyperion Takes a Hit

Surrounded by invisible naked ladies
I haunted alleyways of wrecked organdy.
Listening to Heitor Villa-Lobos's fantasies.

What I like is starter fluid on Bozo's grave.

Demand Eternity (but settle for ecstasy).
Malappropriation Strategies, for instants:
Custard's Last Stand;
20,000 Leaks Under the Sea.

IOUs dripping from the sun's blind spot.

What kind of fuel am I?

My arms still brag about holding you up
in night's watch-repair shop.

Fire lost in your lips I find abandoned.
There are only green lights in Go Town.

Peter the Great

A few clouds in the south proceed apace.
My days are made of such lost parades.

Helen Hooker plays a madrigal on WQXR.
Red coxcombs spout wrinkled flame.

Sunset flares, a halo behind your hair.
Homing geese seek the horizon's navel.

Life is swell and you are a lucky charmer.
The sugar-frosted Snow Moon beams.

Under your spell, on top of *der Welt*.
Submersed in the champagne of your wake.

Your lips touch mine, softly idling, like
a getaway car. Lightning on your breath.

This is what I live for, to be here, inside
the glow only majesty can bequeath.

Spreading the Wealth

Each snowflake is the king of wind,
diving and rising by command,
until landing on snowdrops
who bow pale lavender heads.

You go back and forth between
being blind and seeing into my heart
standing trial in love's court.

But you always come out on top.
Like snow. Embarrassingly beautiful
in your intent at least.
You never promise to compromise
and we are louder than allowed
syncing the dream bundle
with full rounds of empty wonder.

Shame and the Shamans

Speaking of flambeaux, I will be yours.
The night may wiggle but you'll be still
here when next we address the sun.
And get dressed in our investments.

Lost inside a wounded rainbow,
I grub for roots in the ghost meadows.
We need to enunciate our elucidation.
Aye, there's the rubber meeting the road.

My dad's last words were "Oh, Shit."
At least he got that comma in there.
To become our full selves we dissolve
into reams of the dark's unscrolling log.

O, Darling, you were torching the clock
and I was holding on to a lucky hand.

State Mint

A caravan of lost chances staggers on.
Steam calls me to the witness stand.
Your eyes arc weld beams to sundown.

Life plunges, a waterfall we go over
inside a charred whiskey barrel.
Licensed to fool ourselves en masse.

And the species gags on the hand
it's dealt. I need to be alone now:
a lighthouse in Mercury's solarium.

The heart of forever beats me up.
Pigeons fan their tails and ruffle-puff.
Borodin takes us out for a liquid lunch.

Surely there's a better way to play
it cool. Threading what stars unspool.

Cantata

Drought robs the sycamores, plucking
leaves in June. A breeze pushes them

into a swarm of withered pages
rasping anxiously across the court.

Then stillness. They die back down.
Invisible forces carry us along.

I am a prisoner of hope.
A congress of loneliness. A dry tear.

An old motor sputters before purring.
Empty boxcars couple with a boom.

Copying Ovid's playbook, I hold out
for change. Home is made of wings.

Thunder clears its throat but won't sing.
The goal in life is joy. Today sun reigns.

The Ostrich Colony

Born to rhyme: you all hot for posterity
and me in hot pursuit of your posterior.
Even alone we are not wee.

Japonica spills buttons in prim rows.
Virginia bluebells ring the river path.
Elsewhere freedom fighters flail.

Our hour on the promenade we hover,
never landing but ever furthering
a cascading effort that escorts us here.

"So, you want to do it again?" Sure.
Practice makes us purr. Then
black lentils and tarragon for dinner.

Looking underground for what matters.
Time leaves holes to stick our heads in.

Ode to a Nightcap

for Hillary Keel

The last party boat steers for Red Hook,
strings of light webbing its stern,
ghost eyes riveting water's black mirror.

Home is a course we can only channel.
Our nets come back alive with echoes.

I miss you when brute tugs bellow.
When a lusty foghorn bows its cello.
When the Williamsburg Bridge trundles
into slumber, its cables, a giant's harp.

Dream until it hurts, Star Burst.

I've been onto you ever since meeting
at the garden, your smile a beacon.
Here's to you, fairy lover from Vienna.
Until the rabbit and top hat unite as one.

Required Fields

Clouds shuck the sky leaving pearl.
A Chinese woman walks a Welsh dog.
I am a swan and you are becoming
a ladder made of wands. We
believe in the Pirates of Penance.

Detectives search for a missing address.
Friends attend a random protest.
Some of us bet on long shots,
charting a course of emptiness.
Our shoes wear out chasing a dream.

Once, our eyes burned, torturing light.
Remember how we begged for answers?
Now catastrophes are nothing new.
Gratitude never ends. Other things do.

Ask Me

The wolf moon goes down like butter
on our pancakes made with bean flour.
Wind axes white blazes on the black,
brackish Hudson. Daily errands arise:

Transcribing the diary of Minerva's owl;
Adding scarred sparks to fire's engine;
Zeroing in on water's flying roots.

This is where I find you, half hidden
in the bull rushes, naked and alone.
Dirty silence pushes us together,
combing honey from our unity as we

inherit a new berth in every breath.

I know a keeper when one comes along.
Miracles are makeable if you ask me.

Changing Station

Agony—the inevitability of our demise.
We were spinning sugar when the giant
crutch fell short. The clocks running
for their lives. The city humming
like a freezer. A black caboose on ice.

You were making mushroom ragu.
I was admiring your industry, reading
the Metropolitan section. When
the denouement comes, look for me
in the cockpit handing out straws
to clutch at as we veer into a viral spiral.

The Empire State Building's opal spire
cuts into night. That's kinda how
I am now—a lightsaber, ready for hire.

Host and Hostage

Jackdaws gather at 4:27 to wrangle
over afternoon's felt hat.

I listen to Piano Trio No. 1 in E-flat.

A little ocean gargles in my throat,
practicing bad goodbyes.

Somehow I've managed to love
all whom I've known. Curmudgeons
in dank dungeons and giants
in fog cages. Their beautiful wounds
stuffed into bottles, wash up now
like beached stars on hissing sand.

Our suffering is buffered by
the offerings we glean from our trials.

Squeezing forever out of a wile.

Fog's Heavy Crown

I'm on a grand jury. Bells are ringing.
A siren chases bad luck.

Charges are brought up—fates
delivered by our show of hands.

Pouring prayers into a muddy yard,
snowflakes practice disappearing.

Death prepares us to live in solitude's
garage. You are my bumper car.

Let the lonely find each other
like plastic bags snagged on a cross.

I am my own zoo and so are you.
We follow hollow sight into a keyhole.

We come out like red lights throbbing
atop high-rises, crowned by heavy fog.

Salvos

Night rides hard on its quarter moon saddle
chasing a dream through December's froth.

Pounding on tomorrow's backdoor,
I barge into the passageway tracking a whim.

Leaves frozen to the path head for home.
Crinkly carnations stretch cranky truth.

We dither with dust's feathers, ever
grateful for heroes we find in dark spots.

Bernadette's gotten younger since she died,
taking time and scattering it in glitter wind.

My personal goal is to score.
There's some eggnog left and rum from Haiti.

Be my stage and I'll be your coach.
Lick my wounds. Be a salve for love's slave.

Sexistentialism

Daylilies rave, brief candles on a cake.

June was a blip, a blurred face stealing
past strobing slats. A few words
left like ants on our picnic blanket.

Feeding the blaze between your legs
I strode into the winner's circle
like the square root of a lost division.

A witch burning sentences at the stake.

I'm yours, Star Fleece. You flay me.

Venus hot-wired and gasping.

The mattress bucks, doubling as a prow.
Rejoicing in juice. Salting light.

Blotting time with a word countess.
My life, a mandala of thirsty glasses.

Fuel for Love

Sundown drags some fiery slag into a gap
in the Jersey skyline. Day's wick meets
the star trimmer and glides toward
the target area. Harvesting goodbyes.

Old statues vow to obey whatever
green habits they have donned. Shadows
of wigs weave through the parks' limbs.

Windfall plums bruise the ground.
Our story, a road of half-used light.

Welcome to the hero you've squeezed
out of an antique compass.
Checking the mirror, our driver signals.

Now, cashing in the tokens of distance,
what we run on expands as it diminishes.

Tall King Talking

> *concerned with the voltage of angels ...*
> —Will Alexander

A blind pilot, your tongue mixes the point,
busy taking the future's order.

Last Call at Lascaux.
Borneo Again.

You will teach the willows to weep
and turn their tears into carbon sinks.

Keep a star's eyelash on a leash.
Listen to the telemetry of trembling.

A language long entombed in lightning's vault
ignites the vesper fields.

Dust bites its nails. Snails leave their script
on the columbine's green hearts.

For now, there's only the new and the knew,
involuntary spasms drowning the sun's spine.

The Daily News

Across from the library and its mossy bangs,
pigeons flurry, dicing the air.

Caution light caught between red and green,
a golden eye that sees all for a brief reprieve.

Squirrel scrawled on dusk's blackboard
bends the higher branches, not the highest.

I came looking for unlikely glory.
My days carved out of starving pearls.

In the palace of beggars, love is the quarry.
A singing fire we learn how to hurl.

The river's hair sweeps me into your arms.
Let tomorrow fall into the same trap.

Glad to Be of Surface

for Sarah Arvio

It hurts to be in love, day and night.
A crow hails the cold, deserted light.
Branches break off in intense winds.
A thousand petals clog my view.

We talk fonts: Optima meet Weezie.
Small dogs spiral in a noisy yap spat.
I stain the window with a vacant gaze
looking for a tank of laughing gas.

"Don't make a mountain out of a
mole," the spy said. I've gotten ahead
of myself, following your shadow.
Why stop now, so near the end?

Now that you're a cross between
an avant gardenia and a harlequin.

The Wichita Doctors Are Restless

Still waiting to be overturned, we cornered
the market on nervous green energy.

Twister alley, your black robes flare.
Your artificial prayers plague the prairies.
Hold me close, under the hanging tree,
oh, deputy of the pellet court.

Night builds its nest on the window's brow.

Abraham Lincoln is out trick or treating.
The braindead fall for the gag rule,
like unhinged leaves in a leaf chain store.
Like the fall of the Roman Umpire.

A white pumpkin spoofs my bookshelf.

You're running late and message me.
Crazy love is simply, the icing on the gravy.

White Toaster

Rubbing it with a sponge, scrunging off
a splat of roux or a smudge of fudge,
I become Aladdin. Up periscope.

Welcome to the Wishbone Factory.

As you enter please be sure to poke fun
at the funerary arrangements.

Keep knotting the eternal flame
taking refuge in each pupil. You
early indicator of foxhood, you.

When I say jump you ask how? High?
And so I reply, "I'm with you all the way
from Foggy Mountain to Fancy Gap."

Give it up for the colossal fossil policy.
I'll be your heel, if you'll be my Achilles.

Custer's Last Dessert

The hottest record melts on nomad bikini.
A toll on thrills that is drilling in Alaska.
I thought I told you to think for yourself,
Chief Nowhere to Run with Bells On.

Rain on the train window in Eden's slum.
Trees toss golden manes, heading
to their beheading. Angels trespass,
lounging in leather booths at the after party.

What if we had never met? A crimson
tourniquet, the sky with Tourette's, sinks
in the west. "*#@!," you iterated, irate
that fate chose to betray your regiment.

We put bandages on a bleeding clock
that's getting us ready to take forever off.

Placeholder

Ok, Ringleader, how about some Wagner to go
with your group. Invite them over for dinner
one night when the stars are on strike. I mean
to say I'm sorry and hope to make it up to y'all.

A red towhee and the tea pot trade tirades—
who knows what comes over one? But

thanks for including me in your secret sauce.

As we pull into the station, a trace of luster
sticks to the glass and we can see ourselves
looking back like hunted monkeys or jockeys
who ride so fast that time loses its bearings

and flops around like a football. Ok, then! Cool.

You in love with me, tear a page from the wind
and make some room for us to grow wild in.

Calling the Tune

We were wringing pitch from the stars,
making torches for struggling jugglers.

We toasted the breadwinners, may they
be welcomed by every loafer
between here and Tuscaloosa where
old elephants head in spring as rain
sings like lingerie on bowing boughs.

Way to go, sassafras eyes! Did I say
how fine you are, such infinite finesse?

Sometimes the best times are blind—
feeling their way through a feathered cave.
Dancing on waves of chromium fire.

While the world burns let them remember
we did our best to answer to the fiddler.

Nights & Daisies

> *no more paths for us ...*
> —Yves Bonnefoy

Bring your drum, a pile of darkness,
black cherries. Bring a fire you let
go out. Bring your naked trust.

Bring the strait you swim across.
Bring the chain of storms you ride
like a bandit inside. Bring a bottle.

Bring a shoreline to the party.

God has given up trying to finish us.
We're too thirsty for heaven's well.

I hear you splashing in the unknown
river that runs between our legs.

Surrounded by a waterfall of now.

This is my love letter to everything,
written in rain on evening's gown.

Selected Poetry Titles Published by SurVision Books

Contemporary Tangential Surrealist Poetry: An Anthology
Edited by Tony Kitt
ISBN 978-1-912963-44-7

Invasion: An Anthology of Ukrainian Poetry about the War
Edited by Tony Kitt
ISBN 978-1-912963-32-4

Noelle Kocot. *Humanity*
(New Poetics: USA)
ISBN 978-1-9995903-0-7

Marc Vincenz. *Einstein Fledermaus*
(New Poetics: USA)
ISBN 978-1-912963-20-1

Helen Ivory. *Maps of the Abandoned City*
(New Poetics: England)
ISBN 978-1-912963-04-1

Tony Kitt. *The Magic Phlute*
(New Poetics: Ireland)
ISBN 978-1-912963-08-9

Clayre Benzadón. *Liminal Zenith*
(New Poetics: USA)
ISBN 978-1-912963-11-9

Thomas Townsley. *Tangent of Ardency*
(New Poetics: USA)
ISBN 978-1-912963-15-7

Mikko Harvey & Jake Bauer. *Idaho Falls*
(Winner of James Tate Poetry Prize 2018)
ISBN 978-1-912963-02-7

John Bradley. *Spontaneous Mummification*
(Winner of James Tate Poetry Prize 2019)
ISBN 978-1-912963-13-3

Charles Kell. *Pierre Mask*
(Winner of James Tate Poetry Prize 2019)
ISBN 978-1-912963-19-5

Charles Borkhuis. *Spontaneous Combustion*
(Winner of James Tate Poetry Prize 2021)
ISBN 978-1-912963-30-0

Noah Falck and Matt McBride. *Prerecorded Weather*
(Winner of James Tate Poetry Prize 2022)
ISBN 978-1-912963-39-3

Michael Zeferino Spring. *Kahlo's Window*
(Winner of James Tate Poetry Prize 2022)
ISBN 978-1-912963-40-9

Dominique Hecq. *Endgame with No Ending*
(Winner of James Tate Poetry Prize 2022)
ISBN 978-1-912963-42-3

George Kalamaras. *That Moment of Wept*
ISBN 978-1-9995903-7-6

George Kalamaras. *Through the Silk-Heavy Rains*
ISBN 978-1-912963-28-7

Order our books from http://survisionmagazine.com

Printed in the USA
CPSIA information can be obtained
at www.ICGtesting.com
LVHW021845120424
777246LV00002B/406